I0091457

Book Writing Journal

Author Notes Guide

Bill Vincent

Copyright © 2016 by **Bill Vincent**. All rights reserved.

No part of this publication may be reproduced, stored in a retrieval system or transmitted in any way by any means, electronic, mechanical, photocopy, recording or otherwise, without the prior permission of the author except as provided by USA copyright law.

Published by Revival Waves of Glory Books & Publishing
PO Box 596| Litchfield, Illinois 62056 USA
www.revivalwavesofgloryministries.com

Revival Waves of Glory Books & Publishing is committed to excellence in the publishing industry.

Book design Copyright © 2016 by Revival Waves of Glory Books & Publishing. All rights reserved.

Published in the United States of America

Paperback: 978-0692746073

Description

After years of writing many books, I thought it was time to release this journal to help others lay out write the book they have always dreamed of writing.

This book is compiled with all the things you must think of when writing your book. From the title to the conclusion it is all here. If you think you can just sit down and write the perfect book from scratch in the order, it needs to be in, good luck with that. It is smart for any author to take some time and even take notes before actually writing. From beginning to end, you can have a good idea before you actually write your book. Even if you have written a book before, it is a good idea to use this Book Writing Journal to perfect your writing.

Outline Notes

OUTLINE NOTES

OUTLINE NOTES

Introduction Notes

Introduction Notes

Introduction Notes

INTRODUCTION NOTES

Chapter 1 Notes

CHAPTER 1 NOTES

CHAPTER 1 NOTES

Chapter 1 Notes

CHAPTER 2 NOTES

CHAPTER 2 NOTES

CHAPTER 2 NOTES

Chapter 2 Notes

CHAPTER 3 NOTES

CHAPTER 3 NOTES

CHAPTER 3 NOTES

CHAPTER 3 NOTES

CHAPTER 4 NOTES

CHAPTER 4 NOTES

CHAPTER 4 NOTES

CHAPTER 4 NOTES

CHAPTER 5 NOTES

CHAPTER 5 NOTES

Chapter 5 Notes

Chapter 5 Notes

CHAPTER 6 NOTES

CHAPTER 6 NOTES

Chapter 6 Notes

CHAPTER 6 NOTES

CHAPTER 7 NOTES

Chapter 7 Notes

CHAPTER 7 NOTES

CHAPTER 7 NOTES

CHAPTER 8 NOTES

CHAPTER 8 NOTES

CHAPTER 8 NOTES

CHAPTER 8 NOTES

CHAPTER 9 NOTES

CHAPTER 9 NOTES

CHAPTER 9 NOTES

CHAPTER 9 NOTES

CHAPTER 10 NOTES

Chapter 10 Notes

Chapter 10 Notes

Chapter 10 Notes

CONCLUSION NOTES

CONCLUSION NOTES

CONCLUSION NOTES

CONCLUSION NOTES

Extra Notes

Extra Notes

Extra Notes

EXTRA NOTES

EXTRA NOTES

EXTRA NOTES

SYNOPSIS NOTES

Synopsis Notes

Synopsis Notes

BIO NOTES

BIO NOTES

Bio Notes

TITLE & SUB-TITLE NOTES

TITLE & SUB-TITLE NOTES

TITLE & SUB-TITLE
NOTES

Publishing Notes

PUBLISHING NOTES

PUBLISHING NOTES

PUBLISHING NOTES

Marketing Notes

Marketing Notes

MARKETING NOTES

Marketing Notes

www.ingramcontent.com/pod-product-compliance
Lightning Source LLC
Chambersburg PA
CBHW072155020426
42334CB00018B/2018